FUN WITH MAP SKILLS

Hunting

on the MAP

Alix Wood

PowerKiDS
press

New York

Published in 2015 by Rosen Publishing
29 East 21st Street, New York, NY 10010

Copyright © 2015 by the Rosen Publishing Group, Inc.
Produced for Rosen by Alix Wood Books

Editor for Alix Wood Books: Eloise Macgregor
Designer: Alix Wood
US Editor: Joshua Shadowens
Researcher: Kevin Wood
Geography Consultant: Kerry Shepheard, B.Ed (Hons) Geography

Photo credits: all images © Shutterstock

Publisher's Cataloging Data

Wood, Alix.
Hunting on the map / by Alix Wood.
p. cm. — (Fun with map skills)
Includes index.
ISBN 978-1-4777-6980-5 (library binding) — ISBN 978-1-4777-6981-2 (pbk.) —
ISBN 978-1-4777-6982-9 (6-pack)
1. Hunting—Juvenile literature. 2. Navigation—History—Juvenile literature.
3. Maps —Juvenile literature. I. Wood, Alix. II. Title.
SK35.5 W69 2015
910.4—d23

Manufactured in the United States of America

CPSIA Compliance Information: Batch #WS14PK9: For Further Information contact Rosen Publishing, New York, New York at 1-800-237-9932

Contents

Using Maps

If you go hunting you will probably need a map. Maps help to plan your trip and help you work out where you are. A map is a diagram of the Earth's surface. Maps can be of a large area such as a whole country, or a small area such as a woodland. Maps help you know if you are going in the right direction. They can show you where different types of **terrain** are too, such as where the grasslands or mountains are.

Hunters use different types of maps to find the information they need. They may want to look at a world map or a globe to decide which part of the world to hunt in. More often though they would need maps of a smaller area with more detail. A close-up map of a small area is called a small **scale** map. A map of a bigger area is called a large scale map.

▲ Two hunters looking at a small scale map of the forest.

Do You Know?

The Earth is shaped like a ball. Maps of the Earth that are ball-shaped are called globes.

Do You Like Hunting?

Hunting is a sport where people track wild animals. Sometimes hunters kill the animals, but not always. We sometimes hunt animals to track their movements and help protect them, or to photograph them. Some people think that hunting to kill is cruel. Hunting can help keep down the numbers of certain animals in an area. The animals may spread disease, or there may just be too many of them. Hunters will often eat the meat from the animals that they hunt. Wild animals have had a free and natural life, which isn't always true of the farmed animals that we eat.

Maps are usually flat. A flat paper map is much easier to fold and go in your pocket than a globe would be! People who make maps have to turn the curved Earth's surface into a flat drawing. These types of maps are called **projections**. Projections alter the shape of the land a little.

Try Your Skills

1. Which map shows a small area in detail?
   a) small scale   b) large scale

2. Which map is more accurate,
   a) a flat map?   b) a globe?

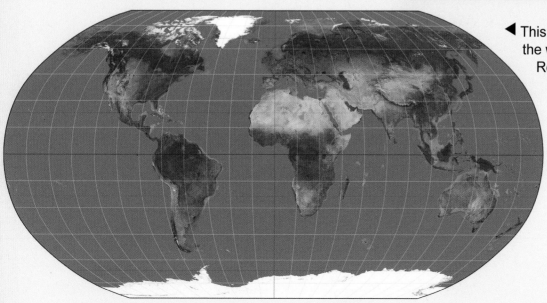

◀ This flat map of the world uses the Robinson projection. It makes the areas of water larger than they really are to keep the size and shape of the land more accurate.

Following Tracks

Animals leave trails that are almost like maps of how to find them! They leave footprints, droppings, and areas of broken branches or bent grass. Scratches on trees are a sign that male deer are around. Tracking is a useful skill for hunters, animal photographers, and anyone wanting to observe animals in the wild.

Look at the animal trail map below. Maps use simple drawings called **symbols** to show you different features on a map. The key tells you what the symbols mean. Look at the symbols and see if you can answer the questions and track down the animals. Good luck!

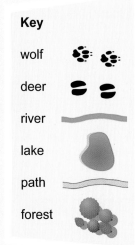

1. Where does the wolf stop to drink?

2. Where do the deer like to hide?

3. Who likes to walk along the paths?

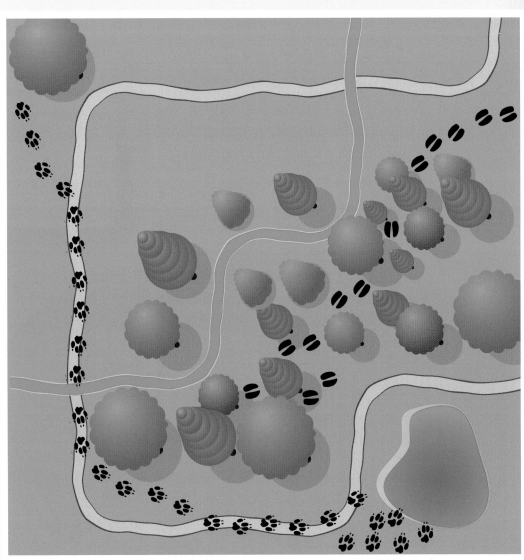

Do You Know?

When you walk, only some parts of your foot touch the ground. A footprint doesn't look exactly like the foot that makes it.

▲ An elk   ▲ An elk's hoof print

How to Track A Wild Animal

1. It's easiest to track in snow, mud, or soft soil.
2. Walk quietly. Wear sneakers. Don't step on twigs. Step from heel to toe to soften your step.
3. Don't wear colorful clothing.
4. If the animal may be dangerous, keep your distance.
5. Have a cellphone, **GPS**, map, and compass with you so you do not get lost.

Make A Plaster Cast Animal Track

You will need some plaster of paris, a bowl, a cup of water, a plastic bottle, and some scissors.

1. Find an animal track. Gently clear the area around it.

2. Ask an adult to cut a 1 inch (2.5 cm) ring out of a plastic bottle. Gently press the plastic ring halfway into the soil around the track. This makes a wall to pour the plaster into.

3. Mix the plaster in the bowl following the packet's instructions. Slowly stir the plaster until it is creamy with no lumps or air bubbles. Gently tap the bowl to make any bubbles come to the top.

4. Pour the plaster around the inside edge of the circle. Let the plaster flow into the track. Fill to the top. Leave the plaster to harden for 30 minutes to an hour.

5. Remove the cast by digging just around the outside and underneath the cast. Lift it carefully. Do not pry the cast out as it may crack. In two days the cast will be dry enough to clean or paint.

Target Practice

A gun sight helps you aim at your target. A gun sight is a little like a compass. A compass helps you find north. A compass has a magnetic needle which will always point to the **north magnetic pole**. Knowing what direction you are facing helps you find your way when you are using a map. When hunting, hitting your target accurately is very important. Target practice is a great way of sharpening up your skills.

▲ A gun sight

▲ A compass

A compass rose is drawn on the compass. The rose shows the points of the compass. The four main **cardinal directions** are north, south, east, and west. They are usually written using just their first letter, N, S, E, and W. On most maps north points to the top of the page.

Try Your Skills

Can you help Hunter Hank by giving him directions? Does Hank need to aim north, south, east, or west toward these animals?

1. the jack rabbit

2. the moose

3. the deer

4. the squirrel

deer

squirrel

jack rabbit

moose

8

Getting More Accurate

Intermediate directions are halfway between the four cardinal directions of north, south, east, and west. The intermediate directions are northeast, northwest, southeast, and southwest. They are usually shortened to NE, NW, SE, and SW. Can you point this target shooter in the right direction to hit each target at the shooting range? Use the compass below to help you.

What direction are these targets from the red circle?

1. target A
2. target B
3. target C

Do You Know?

Compass roses have been drawn on charts and maps since the 1300s!

Mapping the Land

Different types of wild animals like to live in different types of terrain. When you are tracking an animal, it is good to know where they may be. Maps can help with this. **Topographical** maps show an area's mountains and valleys. They will also usually show the roads, trails, rivers, lakes, and types of plant life. All of this information can be very useful on a hunting trip.

mountains

lake

vegetation

A map will have a key explaining what each color or symbol represents. The contour lines will have numbers written on them. These show the height that the line's area is above or below the level of the water in the sea. The height above sea level is sometimes called **elevation**.

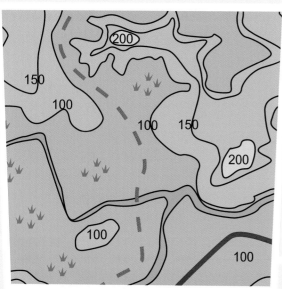

Key

~~~ river

- - - trail

🌱 marshland

—— road

—100— elevation

Look at the map on the left. Can you answer these questions?

1. Is the marshland on flat land or hilly land?

2. Does the trail go up any hills?

3. Does the trail cross the road or the river?

Using Maps To Scout The Area

You are heading out to the area drawn in the map below. You want to photograph some deer. Below are some facts about deer that will be useful when you plan your trip.

- Deer don't usually like walking up hills.
- Deer like to keep hidden in or near woodland.
- Deer don't like the noise from traffic.
- Deer graze on the grasslands

A deer stand is a blind. They are built on tall legs so that the deer won't see you. After reading the facts, which deer stand do you think you should head to?

1. Stand A   2. Stand B
3. Stand C   4. Stand D

Using Aerial Photography

Looking at an aerial image of an area can help plan a hunting trip. An aerial image is a photograph taken from an airplane or a satellite. Aerial images are good at showing plant life, rivers, mountains, and clearings. Topographical maps use symbols to show where a forest is. A satellite image will show you the actual forest, with every tree exactly where it really is. Satellite images are updated often too, so they are usually more up-to-date than a map.

A wolf has escaped from the local wildlife park. Your mission is to help track the wolf and return it to the park. Look at the satellite image and the information about how to track wolves. Would you search in search area 1, 2, or 3?

Tracking Wolves

- Look for birds circling over a fresh wolf kill.

- Look where animals that wolves hunt, such as deer, may live.

- Wolves like the easy path, so look along the trails.

Key

◯ search area 1

◯ search area 2

◯ search area 3

Hunters could divide the search area up into squares. These squares are called a grid. The search team can then search one grid square at a time, and be sure they have not missed any hiding places. To tell someone which square to search, say the number that goes along the grid first ⟶. Then say the number that goes up and down ↑. You can remember the order by saying "walk before you fly."

Do You Know?

You always say the number that belongs to the bottom left hand corner of the grid square.

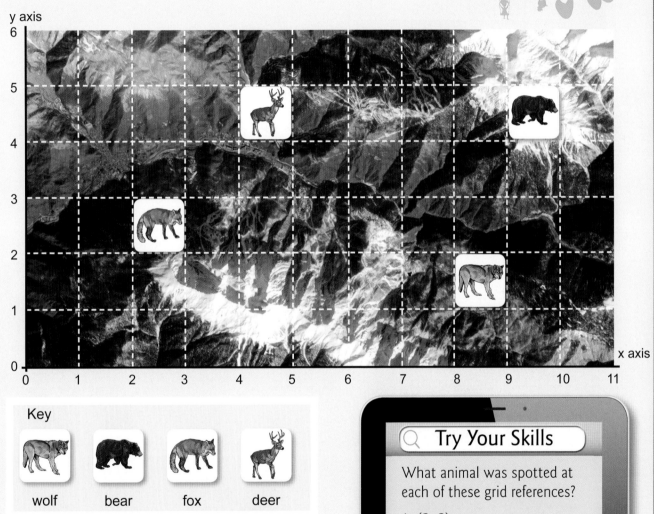

Key

wolf   bear   fox   deer

Local people have seen animals in the mountains. They have marked their sightings with pictures on the grid. Can you answer the questions on the right and help track them down?

Try Your Skills

What animal was spotted at each of these grid references?

1. (2, 2)
2. (9, 4)
3. (8, 1)
4. (4, 4)

13

Hiding in the Jungle

You are tracking animals in the jungle with a guide. Peeking through the bushes, your guide is pointing out the animals to you using grid references or bearings. Can you find all the animals?

🔍 Try Your Skills

What animal is at each of these grid references?

1. (2, 2)	5. (5, 1)
2. (0, 1)	6. (0, 3)
3. (4, 3)	7. (1, 2)
4. (5, 3)	8. (4, 2)

Key

leopard   frogs   butterfly

parrot   spider   toucan   snake

A compass can give you very accurate directions by using compass **bearings**. The compass rose is divided into 360 degrees, just like a circle is in math. Lay a ruler from the red dot in the center of the compass rose to your target. Read the number that the ruler crosses. That is the animal's bearing.

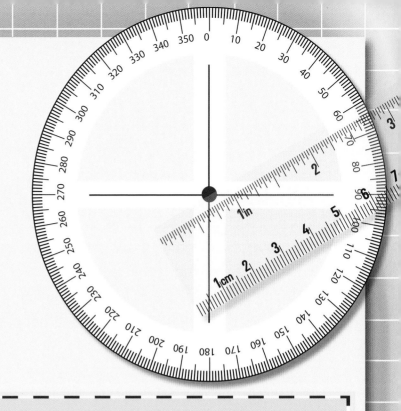

Get Your Bearings

Which animals are at these bearings? Degrees are written like this " °."
1. 330° 2. 0° 3. 38° 4. 300° 5. What bearing is the frog at?

Habitat Maps

Maps can show many different types of information on them. Some maps show different animal **habitats**. A habitat is the type of environment in which animals live. Sometimes the map is marked with pictures of the animals likely to be in each area, such as on the map on the right. Some maps use colored areas to show what the habitat is like, such as the map on page 15. Both type of maps can be helpful for hunters.

An animal needs five things to survive in its habitat. They are food, water, shelter, air, and a place to raise its young. Different animals need different amounts of space. Some animals such as a mountain lion need to roam over a large area. Other animals only need a small space, such as a frog living in a puddle! Once you understand what the animal you are tracking needs, you will be much better able to guess where he may be living.

▲ A 1953 hunting map of the Czech Republic. The map shows where different animals could be found.

Do You Know?

Moose move habitat with the seasons. In spring and early winter moose like open ground. In summer, fall, and late winter they move into the forest.

Match the Habitat Game

Look at these animal information cards. Can you work out which habitat on the map each of the animals should live in?

a) forests b) wetlands c) desert d) prairie

1. Alligator

- Eats fish and animals
- Likes to be on or by water
- Lives in wetlands

2. Coyote

- Eats rats, jackrabbits, reptiles, and vegetation
- Nests in a den
- Lives on the prairie

3. Moose

- Eats vegetation
- Likes shade and trees
- Lives in or near forests

4. Rattlesnake

- Eats mice, rats, and lizards
- Nests in dry, rocky areas
- Lives in deserts

What Is a Scale?

A map is much smaller than the area that it is representing. A **scale** shows you how much smaller it is. A scale can be written in word form. For example it may say "one inch equals 10 miles." Or a map may have a scale drawn on it like the one below. One inch or one centimeter is shown to represent a certain number of miles or kilometers in the real world. On the scale below one inch (2.5 cm) equals one mile (1.6 km).

A scale can be written as a **ratio**. The scale 1:100 means that one unit of measurement on a map is the same as 100 units of measurement in real life. This means that 1 cm on a map represents 1 meter in the real world, or 1 inch on the map represents 100 inches. The bigger the number after the ":" symbol means the larger the area that the map covers.

Try Your Skills

1. Look at the two bears below. One is bigger than the other. Measure each bear's height to their backs. Can you work out what the ratio is?

   a) 1:3 b) 1:2 c) 1:5

2. Which of these maps would show the largest area?

   a) 1:25 b) 1:1,000 c) 1:100

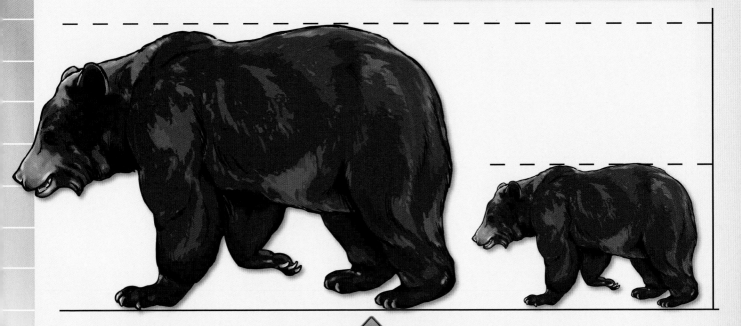

Which Map?

Different scale maps are useful for different hunting expeditions. Look at these three maps of Wildwood Island. Which map would be best for each of the hunting days below?

Go Hunting!

Trip 1.
Find the best cove to go sea fishing from.

Trip 2.
Find the best trail from Huntston to the lake.

Trip 3.
Find the quickest way from the hunting stand to Bear Mountain.

a)

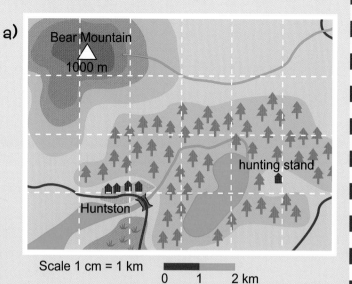

Scale 1 cm = 1 km

0   1   2 km

b)

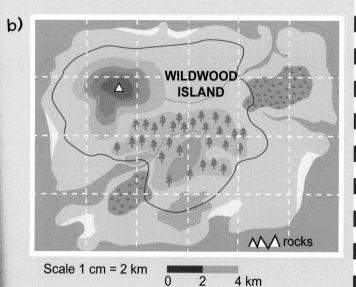

Scale 1 cm = 2 km

0   2   4 km

c)

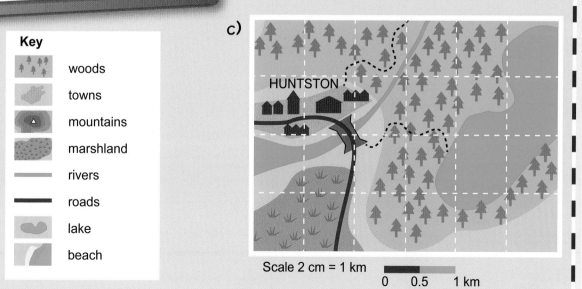

Scale 2 cm = 1 km

0   0.5   1 km

Key

	woods
	towns
	mountains
	marshland
	rivers
	roads
	lake
	beach

Are We There Yet?

Maps can help you work out how far a journey will be. The scale on the map helps you measure the distance. You can use a ruler to measure against the scale if your journey is in a straight line. Use a piece of string along the path if the journey goes around bends. Mark the string at the start and end point of the journey and then measure it against the scale.

wolf

beaver

elk

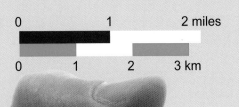

You are on a hunting trip. Look at the map below. You need to walk from the visitor's center along the trails to the hunting areas listed below. How far is each one? Use the scale below to help you. Give your answer to the nearest whole kilometer.

1. the mountain lions
2. the bears
3. the wolves

Do You Know?

Measure from the first dot nearest the visitors center to the last dot nearest the animal. Be careful not to stretch the string.

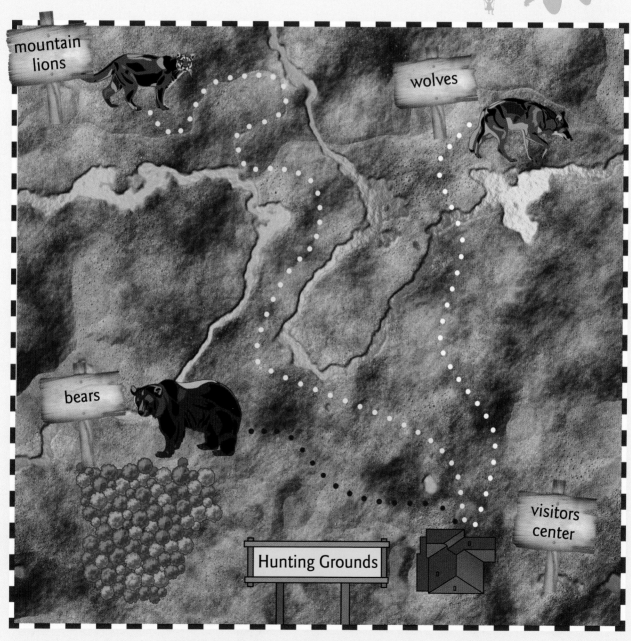

Scale 2 cm = 2 km

0   2   4   6   8   10   12 km

Upwind and Downwind

Animals have an excellent sense of smell. When hunting it is important to know which way the wind is blowing. That way, you can stay upwind of any animals you are trying to hunt and they won't smell you. If you are upwind, the wind blows past the animal toward you. Downwind means the wind blows from you toward the animal. Weather maps will tell you what direction the wind will be blowing.

Wind speed is measured in **knots**. One knot is 1.15 miles (1.85 km) per hour. On weather maps the wind direction is shown using a key symbol. A line points to the direction that the wind is blowing. Lines and triangles along that line show the wind strength. A short line means 5 knots. A long line means 10 knots. A triangle equals 50 knots.

Do You Know?

Winds are always known by the direction they are heading. A northeast wind comes from the southwest and heads northeast.

◀ This wind is blowing northeast at 35 knots. Imagine the symbol is placed on a compass like in the drawing on the right. This will help you work out the wind's direction.

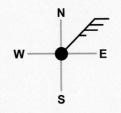

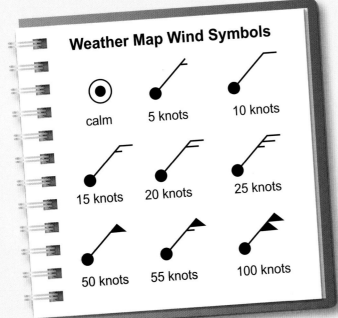

Weather Map Wind Symbols

calm

5 knots

10 knots

15 knots

20 knots

25 knots

50 knots

55 knots

100 knots

Q Try Your Skills

Look at the chart on the left. Can you work out the wind direction and strength of the winds below?

1.

2.

3.

4.

A tracker is in the middle of the forest below. Two animals from the key are in each direction. Can you tell which animals would smell him if the wind blew in these directions?

1. Northwest 3. Southeast
2. East 4. Northeast

Can you find any other animals hiding too?

Make A Wind Detector!

Dry an empty nasal spray bottle and fill it with talcum powder. Gently squeeze the bottle into the air. See which direction the powder is blown.

Key

woodpecker   eagle   skunk   baby bear   bear   deer   wolf   crow

Longitude and Latitude

Different animals live in different parts of the world. A globe can be divided up into lines of **longitude** and **latitude**. Like grid lines, they help people find places on maps. Lines of longitude go from the top to the bottom of a globe. Lines of latitude go across the globe. The lines are numbered, so every place on Earth has its own special number. The position on the lines of latitude is written first, followed by the position on the lines of longitude. A way to remember that is by saying "first, go up or down the rungs of a ladder-tude!"

The prime meridian is 0° longitude. Any lines of longitude heading west from the prime meridian are written with a W after them. Any lines of longitude heading east have an E after them. The equator is 0° latitude. Lines of latitude north or south of the equator have an N or an S after them.

The equator is 0° latitude.

The prime meridian is 0° longitude.

Try Your Skills

Can you answer these questions, Use the globe above to help you.

1. This polar bear cub lives at 66°N. Is that north or south of the equator?

2. Penguins can be found at 72°S. Is that north or south of the equator?

East or West? North or South?

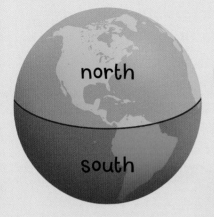
north
south

The equator separates the Earth into two **hemispheres**. The northern hemisphere is above the equator and the southern hemisphere is below. The prime meridian separates the Earth into the western and eastern hemispheres.

west   east

Look at the animal map below. Which hemisphere is each animal found in?

1. What animals are found in the northern hemisphere?

2. What animals are found in the eastern hemisphere?

3. Which animals are in both?

Mountain Lion   Tiger   Leopard

Jaguar   Iberian Lynx   Lion

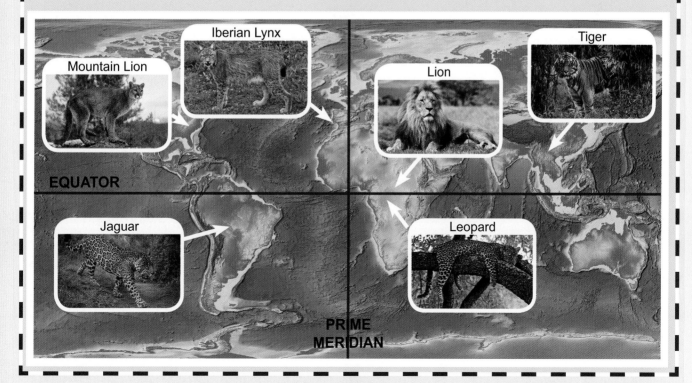
Iberian Lynx
Mountain Lion
Lion
Tiger
EQUATOR
Jaguar
Leopard
PRIME MERIDIAN

What Belongs on a Map?

People that make accurate maps are called cartographers. Some maps, such as the type that help you find your way at a fun park, are not that accurate. Most accurate maps will have a title, scale, key, compass rose, and grid on them. Have a look at some maps and see if you can find all of these features on them.

The title says what the map shows, for example whether it is a street map or one showing vegetation. The key tells the reader what the symbols on the map represent. The compass rose shows the compass points. Sometimes a map just shows which way is north, instead. The scale translates distances shown on the map into distances on the ground. There may also be a grid over the map, to help locate places.

Try Your Skills

1. Look at the map below. The cartographer who made this map forgot to put something on it. Can you work out which it is?

   a) title   d) scale

   b) key   e) grid

   c) compass

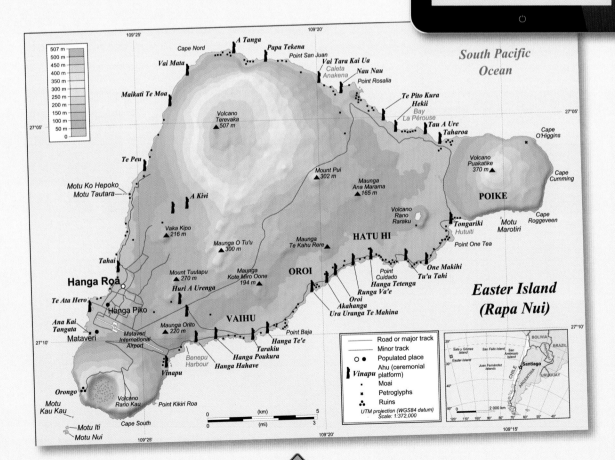

Make Your Own Hunting Map Game

You will need a friend, a large piece of paper, some small pieces of paper, pens, and tape.

1. Find somewhere outdoors where you can find some animals. Measure out an area 10 paces by 10 paces.

2. Measure a 10 inch (25.5 cm) square on the large piece of paper. Draw a grid of 1 inch (2.5 cm) squares on the map.

3. Draw your map. Put in features such as any water, grassy or sandy areas, stones, or burrows.

4. Write the name of any animals that you have seen on the small pieces of paper.

Try this game. Get your map and pieces of paper and go out to the hunting area. When you find any animals, tape that name onto the right area on the map. Leave the animals where you find them and try not to scare them away. Then go back and find a friend. Give her the map and see if she can find all the animals using your map.

Do You Know?

Put a title, scale, compass, key, and grid onto your map. Your scale will be 1 inch (2.5 cm) = 1 pace.

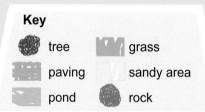

Key
- tree
- paving
- pond
- grass
- sandy area
- rock

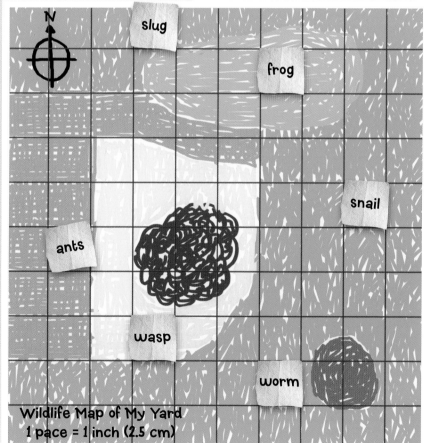

Wildlife Map of My Yard
1 pace = 1 inch (2.5 cm)

slug
frog
snail
ants
wasp
worm

Tracking Using Satellite

A global positioning system (GPS) is a system of **satellites** and **receivers**. GPS is what a car's satellite navigation uses to know its position. GPS can be used by people to track animals. A transmitter tag is placed on the animal. The tag gives off a signal. A satellite receiver can pick up the signal and work out exactly where the animal is.

Satellite networks have tracked the movements of many different animals. Florida manatees are an **endangered** species. They need protection. Radio tracking showed that Florida manatees travel much further up the Atlantic Coast of the United States than scientists had thought. This information means that the scientists can help protect the manatees by watching those areas of the sea for any polution dangers, too.

Do You Know?

How do you put a tracker on an animal? Trackers can be put on a collar, on a harness, glued onto feathers or skin, or attached onto an animals's horns!

GPS systems can be used to track animals. The GPS tags send out a signal with the animal's latitude and longitude location. Scientists can use this information to understand the animals better. Scientists tracking sea turtles have discovered that female sea turtles will always return to the beach where they were born to lay their own eggs! The green sea turtle swims around 1,400 miles (2,253 km) between feeding grounds and nesting sites!

Tracking Turtles

Look at this turtle's journey on the map. The turtle starts his journey on the April 1, at 21°N, 170°W. Follow its route on the map and then answer the questions.

1. What latitude and longitude is the beach that the turtle stopped at?

2. Did the turtle ever swim south?

3. How many days was the turtle traveling?

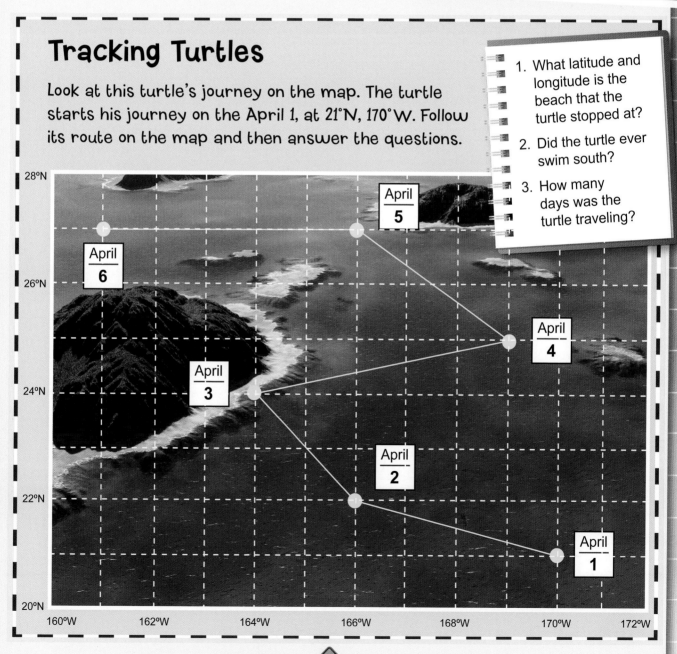

Glossary

bearings (BER-ingz)
The positions or directions of one point with respect to another or to the compass.

cardinal directions (KAHRD-nul dih-REK-shunz)
One of the four principal points of the compass: north, south, east, west.

compass rose (KUM-pus ROHZ)
A drawing on a map which shows directions.

contour lines (KON-toor LYNZ)
Lines (as on a map) connecting the points that have the same elevation on a land surface.

elevation (eh-luh-VAY-shun)
The height to which something is raised.

endangered (in-DAYN-jerd)
Threatened with extinction.

GPS (JEE-PEE-ES)
GPS is short for global positioning system. GPS devices tell you your exact position by using information from orbiting satellites.

habitat (HA-buh-tat)
The type of place where an animal naturally lives.

hemispheres (HEH-muh-sfeerz)
The halves of the Earth as divided by the equator or by a meridian.

intermediate direction (in-ter-MEE-dee-et dih-REK-shun)
Northeast, northwest, southeast, or southwest.

latitude (LA-tih-tood)
Distance north or south from the equator measured in degrees.

longitude (LON-jih-tood)
Distance measured by degrees or time east or west from the prime meridian.

north magnetic pole (NORTH mag-NEH-tik POHL)
The direction of the earth's magnetic pole, to which the north-seeking pole of a magnetic needle points when free from local magnetic influence.

projections (pruh-JEK-shunz)
A method of showing a curved surface (as the earth) on a flat one (as a map).

ratio (RAY-shoh)
The relationship in quantity, amount, or size between two or more things.

receivers (rih-SEE-verz)
Equipment for receiving radio or television signals.

satellites (SA-tih-lyts)
A man-made object or vehicle intended to orbit the earth, the moon, or another heavenly body.

scale (SKAYL)
Size in comparison.

symbols (SIM-bulz)
Drawing that stand for real things.

terrain (tuh-RAYN)
The surface features of an area of land.

topographical
(tah-puh-GRA-fih-kul)
A map that shows the heights and depths of the features of a place.

Read More

Besel, Jennifer M. *Compass Rose and Directions*. Mankato, MN: Capstone Press, 2014.

Quinlan, Julia J. *GPS and Computer Maps*. New York: PowerKids Press, 2012.

Shea, Robert Kennedy. *Hunting*. New York: Gareth Stevens, 2013.

Due to the changing nature of Internet links, PowerKids Press has developed an online list of websites related to the subject of this book. This site is updated regularly. Please use this link to access the list:

www.powerkidslinks.com/fwms/hunt/

Index

Answers

page 5
1. a, 2. b
page 6
1. lake, 2. forest, 3. wolf
page 8
1. east, 2. south, 3. north,
4. west
page 9
1. northwest, 2. north,
3. northeast
page 10
1. flat land, 2. no, 3. river
page 11
1. Stand B

page 12
search area 2
page 13
1. fox, 2. bear, 3. wolf,
4. deer
page 14
1. parrot, 2. frog, 3. spider,
4. toucan, 5. snake, 6.
butterfly, 7. frog, 8. leopard
page 15
1. leopard, 2. butterfly,
3. toucan, 4. spider, 5. 20°
page 17
1. b, 2. d, 3. a, 4. c

page 18
1. b, 2. b
page 19
1. b, 2. c, 3. a
page 20
1. elk, 2. beaver
page 22
1. 10 knots northeast,
2. 50 knots north,
3. 25 knots southwest,
4. 35 knots northeast
page 23
1. crow, wolf, 2. deer,
woodpecker, 3. skunk,

baby bear, 4. bear,
eagle
page 24
1. north, 2. south
page 25
1. mountain lion,
iberian lynx, lion,
tiger, 2. lion, tiger,
leopard, 3. lion, tiger
page 26
1. c
page 29
1. 24N, 164W
2. no, 3. 5 days